TELLY ADDICT

COP SHOWS

TELLY ADDICT

COP SHOWS

First published in the UK in 2014

© Demand Media Limited 2014

www.demand-media.co.uk

Printed and bound in Europe

ISBN 978-1-910270-06-6

Contents

Introduction

Cop shows have enjoyed a prominent place in broadcasting since the early days of television. *Telly Addict: Cop Shows* highlights

more than 50 popular shows that have given pleasure to audiences since the birth of the medium. The variety of shows ranges from gritty urban dramas like *The Bill* and *The Sweeney* to lighthearted spoofs such as the outrageous *Police Squad!*, with everything from *A Touch of Frost*, *T.J. Hooker*, *Charlie's Angels*, *Hawaii 5-0*, *Inspector Morse*, *The Saint* and *Z-Cars* in between. Stars like Sylvester Stallone, Dennis Farina, Samuel Jackson and Tom Selleck launched their careers in cop shows, while many like David Jason, John Thaw, Nick Berry, Martin Shaw, Maud Adams, Stephanie Turner and Jodie Foster cemented their reputations as the finest actors of their generation having been cast in the most iconic television dramas of the last 60 years.

TELLY ADDICT : **COP SHOWS**

America's Most Wanted

Two European TV shows – the German *File Reference XY... Unsolved* and the UK's *Crimewatch* – provided the inspiration for *America's Most Wanted*. The German program had already been running for 20 years when Fox executive Stephen Chao and producer Michael Linder proposed the US version.

The premise for the show was that crimes of all kinds – rape, murder, robbery, gang violence, terrorism etc – would be re-enacted with low-budget realism in the hope that viewers would recognise the incident and/or the people involved. They could then call the studio to help police identify the perpetrator(s).

John Walsh was chosen to host the show as his young son had been kidnapped and murdered six years earlier. This gave him a presence and credibility that other candidates couldn't match. *America's Most Wanted* premiered in February 1988 and within four days it achieved an incredible result: David James Roberts, a serial rapist and murderer who was one of the FBI's most wanted criminals, was captured on Staten Island. This convinced the network to expand the show's reach nationwide.

The show continued to achieve startling results as some criminals were apprehended before the credits on that episode had rolled, but production costs then started to escalate and it was briefly cancelled in 1996. However, poor ratings for the shows that replaced *AMW* and an outcry from governors of 37 states forced Fox to reconsider. *AMW* was recalled to Saturday night primetime and its 1000th episode aired in March 2010. In the special, Walsh interviewed Barack

Obama at the White House to discuss his stance on crime.

The show moved to Lifetime in 2011 after Fox pulled the plug, but high royalties then forced the new network to drop *AMW* in early 2013 after nearly 1,200 episodes had aired and a similar number of criminals had been captured.

A Touch of Frost

B ritish police drama *A Touch of Frost* was initially based on the novels by R.D. Wingfield. Produced by Yorkshire TV and then ITV from 1992 until 2010, the series starred David Jason – better known as Del Trotter from *Only Fools and Horses* – as Inspector William Edward 'Jack' Frost, an experienced and driven detective who often clashed with colleagues. Indeed the part helped Jason move away from the richly comic characters he had played before, particularly Del Boy, but also Granville from *Open all Hours* (alongside Ronnie Barker).

The setting for the drama was the fictional town of Denton in Oxfordshire, although most of the outdoor location filming was shot in West Yorkshire. Wingfield's rather coarse and emotionally detached detective was portrayed a little more sensitively by Jason, although, as is common in television series of this kind, the character's skill and dedication to duty are often offset by little foibles and other human failings that are exaggerated for dramatic effect. Indeed the respect he had from colleagues offered a counterpoint to the flaws in his character.

His immediate superior and the target of his jibes was the straight-laced Superintendent Norman Mullett, played by Bruce Alexander whose previous credits included *Keeping Up Appearances*, *Midsomer Murders* and a bit part as the captain of HMS *Chester* in the Bond film *Tomorrow Never Dies*. Mullett admired Frost's tenacity and insight but frequently threatened to relieve him from duty, until Frost broke the case of course. The fact that Frost was awarded a George Cross after being shot meant

that – as the chief constable's favourite officer – he was never likely to be sacked anyway.

Such was the popularity of the series that it endured for 18 years and 42 episodes, as well as being sold to international broadcasters in 19 countries.

Bergerac

Bergerac was a British television series set on the Channel Island of Jersey. It starred John Nettles as Jim Bergerac, a detective with the Jersey police who worked in the fictional foreigners' office and dealt with non-residents of the island.

Producer Robert Stewart had been working on another series (*Shoestring*) with Trevor Eve but the actor then decided to concentrate on theatre work so the series ended abruptly. Stewart proposed filling the slot with a new series based in the Channel Islands – which could draw on plots involving tax exiles and other shady businessmen in a rather more exotic location than Bristol – and the BBC agreed.

Bergerac needed to be easily identifiable and receive the public's sympathy so he was introduced as having been through a traumatic divorce that had seen him turn to the bottle. During a surveillance operation he gave chase to a suspect and broke his leg while intoxicated, and it is against this background that he returned to Jersey from England.

Bergerac had many relationships, including the customary on/off with ex-wife Deborah, as well as liaisons with women who were involved in the plots. Deborah's father, Charlie Hungerford (played by Terence Alexander) appeared in all but one of the 87 episodes, and indeed, somewhat suspiciously, the loveable rogue seemed to be involved to varying degrees in every investigation.

Two of the most popular aspects of the show were Bergerac's 1947 Triumph Roadster and the inclusion of recurring character Philippa Vale (Liza Goddard), a glamorous jewel thief who usually tried

to steal Bergerac's heart. Indeed the best episodes were arguably those which gave the two enough time for their on-screen chemistry to drive the action.

As primary filming was completed on the little island, the locations are easy to find. One would become infamous long after the series had finished, however. The Bureau des Étrangers was actually the Haut de la Garenne, the former children's home that became the centre of attention in a child abuse scandal in 2008. The final show was broadcast on Boxing Day in 1991 after a decade on air.

The Bill

A pilot for *The Bill* was written by novice screenwriter Geoff McQueen in 1983. He saw it as a one-off drama but Michael Chapman at Thames Television was so impressed with the show – rechristened *Woodentop* – that a series was commissioned. The name of the series then reverted to *The Bill*. The first three seasons saw a stable format of an hour-long post-watershed episode per week but such was its popularity that two 30-minute episodes per week were introduced from 1988, which was upped to three in 1993. Five years later it was cut back to an hour per week but then a second hour-long episode was added to ITV's scheduling.

The new format ushered in a soap-opera style whereby the standalone episode was exchanged for a series where plotlines remained ongoing and some characters came and went. A fire at London's fictional Sun Hill police station in 2002 was a simple way to axe many stalwarts from the show but it allowed more plausible characters to be introduced. It also enabled the writers to explore the relationships between officers and their families rather than between each other and the criminals they were trying to apprehend. It also introduced a station that reflected the growing number of ethnic minorities enlisting with the police, as well as broaching more adult themes such as homosexuality in the workplace.

The standalone format was resurrected in 2005 so that the writers could concentrate on individual aspects of serious crime but this only lasted until 2010, by which time ITV felt that viewing tastes had changed and there

was no longer a place for *The Bill* in their schedule. After 2,400 episodes had been broadcast across the UK and transmitted to 55 countries, Britain's longest-running police drama was axed.

In much the same way as *Neighbours* in Australia, the show launched the careers of some of the best-know actors on British television. It also spawned a number of spinoffs, notably *Burnside*, which featured no-nonsense hard-man Christopher Ellison in the title role.

Blue Bloods

Blue Bloods is an American police drama set in New York. Creators Robin Green (*The Sopranos, Southland*) and Mitchell Burgess (*Northern Exposure, Mr. & Mrs. Smith*) based the show around the Reagan family: Frank (Tom Selleck) is the NYPD Police Commissioner; his son Danny (Donnie Wahlberg) is a detective; daughter Erin (Bridget Moynahan) is an assistant DA in Manhattan; youngest son Jamie (Will Estes) is a law graduate who has just joined the police; while dad Henry (Len Cariou) is a retired commissioner.

Frank, a Vietnam veteran with the Marine Corps, is a widower who also lost another son, Joe, in the line of duty. Joe and the FBI were investigating police corruption and were closing in on the suspects when the cops about to be implicated murdered him. Jamie follows up on his brother's investigation and the Reagan family eventually bring the corrupt cops to justice.

The pilot proved extremely popular, with 15 million tuning in, although later shows attracted an average of 13 million, the first scripted Friday night series to manage this in a decade. Reviewers and fans have praised the location shooting and Selleck's performance in particular. The dinner scenes where the family discuss complex and controversial issues have also garnered critical acclaim. So far, the four seasons have produced 86 episodes, and the series looks set to run for the foreseeable future.

Blue Heelers

Blue Heelers was an Australian drama that followed the lives of officers from the fictional Mount Thomas Police Station in rural Victoria. The series was created by Hal McElroy, produced by Southern Star for Channel Seven and ran for 13 years (1993-2006) and 510 episodes.

McElroy first suggested the idea for the show having heard that a friend was training to become a policeman even though he was only 18. He looked into the demographics and discovered that 55% of officers were under the age of 25. This prompted him to investigate why there was such interest in becoming a police officer. When his friend then left the force after a shooting, he realised there could be some substance to a story whereby a city cop transferred to a smaller community after an incident.

Blue Heelers drew worldwide critical acclaim for its realism, particularly the way in which rookies were thrown into challenging situations, and it was eventually broadcast in 108 countries. It also helped launched the careers of major stars like Hugh Jackman. Only Julie Nihill who played Chris Riley, and John Wood who portrayed Tom Croydon, appeared in every episode.

Much like *The Bill*, the series followed the domestic and occupational lives of officers, with each episode being presented from their viewpoint rather than the criminals'. (Channel Seven had initially been presented with two pilots, one of which was shot from the officers' point of view and the other from the criminals'. The network preferred the format of the former.)

Although the setting was small-town

Victoria and most of the cases involved trivial land disputes and petty crime, Mount Thomas had its fair share of kidnappings, armed robberies and murders, as well as the odd terrorist bombing. Whenever a crisis escalated, the Heelers could call in Inspector Russell Falcon-Price from nearby St David's, although his primarily antagonistic role saw him repeatedly threaten to close Mount Thomas Police Station.

Ratings were initially good as the show attracted 2-3 million viewers, but by 2003 the series was feeling a little tired and the production team decided to introduce a new storyline to boost their audience. Mount Thomas Police Station was bombed and several characters were killed off. The small-town innocence had been shed for a darker and grittier series that dealt with more adult themes. The revamp worked for a while but Channel Seven eventually pulled the plug in 2006.

Bones

In an unusual reversal, 20th Century Fox approached screenwriter Hart Hanson about a possible forensic science show in 2004. It transpired that executive producer Barry Josephson had bought the rights to make a documentary on forensic anthropologist and author Kathy Reichs, so some of her work was used as the basis for the series.

Bones draws on an alliance between FBI Special Agent Seeley Booth (David Boreanaz) and forensic anthropologist Doctor Temperance 'Bones' Brennan (Emily Deschanel), who is also the lead character in Reichs's novels. The straight-laced and somewhat socially inept Brennan works at the fictional Jeffersonian Medico-Legal Laboratory, which is closely affiliated with the FBI (in much the same way as the real Smithsonian Institution). Cases involve the examination of human remains, which usually leads to intricate subplots, with Brennan and her team looking at the forensic science while Booth heads up the criminal investigation. Booth has no training in criminology but as a decorated military veteran he analyses people's behaviour and follows his instincts.

The chemistry between the two works particularly well because Brennan is a woman of science rather than God, while Booth is more open-minded and a man of faith. They begin a relationship at the end of the sixth season, have a child in season seven and marry in season nine.

Despite being set primarily in Washington, DC, the show is filmed in Los Angeles. It manages to balance the hard reality of murder investigations with an undercurrent of dark humour that helps relieve tension and adds realism.

Perhaps because of this, the show has been praised as being a sexed-up CSI and often attracts 10 million viewers in the US. It has recently been renewed for a 10th season, which will see the series top 200 episodes.

Cagney & Lacey

Cagney & Lacey was first proposed as a female buddy cop film by producer Barney Rosenzweig. His wife convinced him that there had never been such a film and that it was time to air a series that tackled crime in New York City from a female perspective. Avedon & Corday provided a script but studios weren't keen to take the project. Rosenzweig whittled it down and tried the TV networks instead, but only CBS showed any interest.

Loretta Swift was cast as Christine Cagney for the introductory movie but she had to decline the part fulltime when the *M★A★S★H* production team refused to let her out of her contract. Meg Foster was chosen for the initial series instead, but Sharon Gless replaced her for series two because audiences felt she was too unladylike. Tyne Daly played Mary Beth Lacey.

The TV movie had been praised by critics so the first series was expected to do well after its premier in March 1982. However, although viewers were impressed with the storylines and character development, they found Meg Foster's Cagney too aggressive and CBS cancelled the show after just six episodes.

Thankfully for Rosenzweig, Sharon Gless's sitcom *House Calls* was then axed by Universal and Gless became available. Rosenzweig then managed to persuade CBS to reconsider by promising to tone down the aggression and portray the pair as more feminine. His gamble worked and *Cagney & Lacey* was given a last-minute reprieve.

Poor ratings forced CBS to cancel the show for a second time at the end of the second series. By then, however, it had

a cult following and fans campaigned (successfully as it turned out) to keep it on air. As a last throw of the dice, CBS switched its time slot and ratings suddenly improved. When Tyne Daly received an Emmy nomination (which she then won), the show was brought back mid-season.

Over the next five years the show received another 35 Emmy nominations (14 of which were won) but competition for airtime against *thirtysomething*, *Wiseguy* and *Crime Story* eventually led to its cancellation in 1988. Gless and Daly reunited for four TV movies in the 1990s, and, in 2009, all 125 episodes were made available to download.

C.A.T.S. Eyes

In 1980, ITV aired a police drama with a female lead for the first time. *The Gentle Touch* starred Jill Gascoine as Detective Inspector Maggie Forbes and, aside from dealing with routine police procedures, it also tackled contemporary issues such as racism, mental health problems and homophobia. It was low on action and violence, focusing instead on character-driven plots in a male-oriented world. The series was a huge hit – it regularly drew more than 15 million viewers – and ran for four years (five seasons) and 56 episodes.

The series came to an end in 1984 but there was demand for Maggie Forbes to return, so creator Terence Feely submitted a proposal for a new, more action-oriented show to ITV. *C.A.T.S. Eyes* joined Forbes after she'd left the police to join the Eyes Detective Agency in Kent, although this was actually a front for a Home Office investigative team (Covert Activities Thames Section). Aside from Forbes, the only other character to appear in both *The Gentle Touch* and *C.A.T.S. Eyes* was her love interest, D.I. Mike Turnbull (Bernard Holley).

The first series aired on UK television on Friday nights from April 1985. The second and third series were moved to Saturday nights but this didn't affect what were already strong ratings. The show was eventually axed after three seasons and 30 episodes in June 1987.

Charlie's Angels

Charlie's Angels was an American crime drama created by Ivan Goff and Ben Roberts, and produced by Aaron Spelling. It followed the lives of three graduates from the Los Angeles Police Academy who, when they're only offered menial work for the force, sign up with the Townsend Private Detective Agency run by the mysterious Charlie. The format was the tried-and-tested procedural drama in which a crime was committed, the Angels were sent undercover to solve the case, and they then returned to Charlie to bask in the glory of a job well done.

Three female leads were initially chosen: Kate Jackson played Sabrina Duncan, an intelligent and driven divorcee who was the unofficial leader of the team; Farrah Fawcett played Jill Munroe, athletic, charismatic and a part-time racing driver; and Jaclyn Smith played Kelly Garrett, the tough orphan with a soft centre.

The show was to have been called *The Alley Cats* but Jackson suggested they be called angels instead, and she also recommended that their boss, Charlie, should remain anonymous. Both changes were accepted by producers and proved inspired. Viewers loved the little quirks and the series proved to be a huge hit in its first season. However, there were problems behind the scenes: the three leads were suddenly propelled into the big league and constant demand for photo shoots, wardrobe fittings and interviews left their relationships strained. Fawcett particularly found the attention difficult and, when she felt the quality of the scripts was declining, she left the show.

Cheryl Ladd was cast as her sister, Kris,

and, despite concerns that Fawcett had been the main reason for the high viewing figures, the second series nearly matched the success of the first. But Jackson and Ladd had an extremely fraught off-screen relationship so Shelley Hack was then cast as Jackson's replacement, Tiffany Welles. Hack's performance was roundly criticised however, and the show lost 40% of its viewers. Hack was replaced by model and dance instructor Tanya Roberts who was expected to bring some of the overt sexuality back. The ratings didn't recover though and the show was axed in 1981 after five series and 110 episodes.

A big-budget action film starring Cameron Diaz, Drew Barrymore and Lucy Liu (2000) reignited interest in the franchise, and the 2003 sequel also broke box-office records, but a 2011 TV series without big-name stars was axed almost immediately after critics panned the acting, lack of plot and poor action sequences.

Charlie Chan

Charlie Chan was conceived by Earl Derr Biggers while he was visiting Hawaii in 1919. The novelist had encountered stereotypical racism over the Yellow Peril attitude towards the Chinese and, having read about the exploits of local policemen Chang Apana and Lee Fook, he decided to buck the trend and create an amiable but overweight detective who initially appeared to pose no threat, the polar opposite of traditional Chinese characters like Fu Manchu.

Charlie Chan first appeared in the 1925 novel *The House Without A Key*, although he wasn't central to the plot. A film version was released the following year with Japanese actor George Kuwa playing Chan. Several more films were produced in the late 1920s but none was particularly successful and it wasn't until Swedish actor Warner Oland took the role that Chan became more prominent in the films. By 1938 he'd made 15 movies and the character had at last reached a wider and more appreciative audience.

Charlie Chan's exploits remained popular in a variety of guises – Spanish and Chinese adaptations in particular, as well as via the medium of radio – throughout the 1930s and '40s. There have also been many television versions, and the character has spawned comics and merchandise the world over.

The character himself remains controversial: with his accommodating personality, keen insight and humility, he is viewed as both a positive role model and a brilliant detective who bridges the gap between China and the United States, but others argue that Chan is merely the stereotypical Chinese detective that Biggers thought he'd managed to avoid.

CHiPs

Rick Rosner was working as a reserve deputy for the Los Angeles County Sheriff's department when he had an idea for a buddy police drama. He wrote a treatment and took it to MGM Studios and, in 1977, they agreed to fund a series that followed the lives of two motorcycle officers of the California Highway Patrol (CHP). Rosner saw it as a lightweight action comedy that played on the relationship between macho officer Francis 'Ponch' Poncherello (Erik Estrada) and by-the-book Jon Baker (Larry Wilcox).

As motorcycle cops rarely rode together, the original plots had the accident-prone Poncherello on probation. The pair would generally be assigned a routine patrol and told to look out for various criminals operating in the area. They would then get drawn into a case, which they would solve using a mixture of Baker's wits, Poncherello's muscle and both of their motorbikes. To make the show more appealing to younger audiences, neither man ever drew his firearm (although they did in the TV reunion special *ChiPs 99*).

Erik Estrada couldn't ride a motorcycle when he was cast in the show so he underwent an intensive training course, although he never actually held a licence during the show's six-year 139-episode run. Larry Wilcox was a competent rider and did many smaller stunts, as did Estrada when he was comfortable on the big bikes. Estrada in particular endured more than his fair share of tumbles. While filming season three in 1979 he fell from the bike and broke several ribs and both wrists, so his hospital stay had to be written in to the plot.

The show was on borrowed time when Estrada briefly resigned over syndication profits, and then Wilcox left over a perceived favouritism by producers towards Estrada. The final episode was broadcast in 1983.

Cold Case

Meredith Stiehm was apparently at a TV writing seminar in 2002 when the subject of a cold case series was mentioned. In Canada, a show called *Cold Squad* was already in its fourth season so Stiehm supposedly decided to adapt the idea for American audiences (there is now a legal dispute underway as to whether Stiehm borrowed too directly from *Cold Squad*).

The CBS-backed police procedural drama that resulted saw homicide detective Lilly Rush (Kathryn Morris) of the Philadelphia Police Department re-open several 'cold' cases that were no longer actively being investigated by the fictional department. Episodes usually began with the discovery of a new lead into an old case. Rush then pieced together the evidence and, through interviews with witnesses and traditional detective work, zeroed in on the killer. Episodes ended with the spirit of the victim achieving peace after the capture of their assailant.

The show first aired on Sunday nights in 2003 and it quickly cemented its place in the CBS schedule. The first few seasons attracted 15 million viewers but by its fifth year the series was feeling a little formulaic. It struggled through a couple more years but CBS refused to renew the show for season eight. Despite receiving three Emmys and numerous other awards, *Cold Case* was axed in May 2010 after 156 episodes.

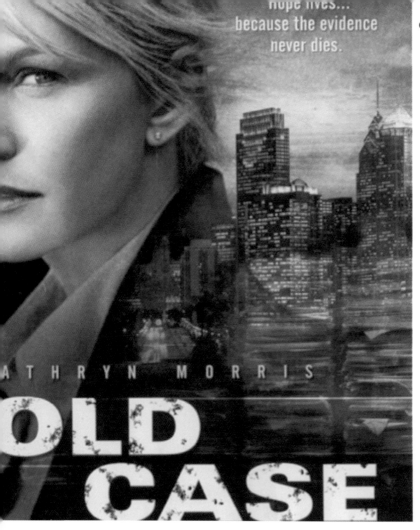

hope lives...
because the evidence
never dies.

ATHRYN MORRIS

OLD CASE

Columbo

William Link and Richard Levinson's classic detective series first aired in 1968, although the character, based loosely on Porfiry Petrovich from *Crime and Punishment* and G.K. Chesterton's Father Brown, had appeared in an episode of *The Chevy Mystery Show* in 1960. Levinson and Link then adapted the drama into a play, *Prescription: Murder*, which debuted in San Francisco two years later. In 1968 the same story was filmed for NBC with Peter Falk as Columbo (Lee Cobb and Bing Crosby both turned it down).

The film was a success so NBC commissioned a pilot for a possible series. The result was the 1971 film *Ransom for a Dead Man*, which was also well received. NBC promptly ordered a 70- or 90-minute show per week, but Falk was unable to commit to such a gruelling shooting schedule so the team reached a compromise whereby they would deliver one episode a month.

The format was unusual in that the classic whodunit was exchanged for the audience seeing the murder happen. Having been assigned to the case, Columbo brought his unique style to the investigation: he was polite, had a keen intellect and good taste, although he always wore his rumpled raincoat, smoked cigars and never divulged his first name. Falk provided his own clothes for the part and it was also his idea to adlib some of the famous Columbo-isms to keep co-stars off balance (he felt it added to the realism and often contributed to their exasperated replies).

Columbo approached each case with a mix of apparent casual absentmindedness and distracting observations, but, despite

his constant probing of suspects, he lulled most into a false sense of security and even appeared to be deliberately putting himself at a disadvantage in the tense exchanges with the killers. Columbo usually left these scenes with the suspect on steady ground but he then asked one more pertinent question to catch them off guard and reveal more about the murder. As each killer manipulated evidence at the scene and then fabricated elaborate cover stories or alibis, Columbo had to sift through a mass of conflicting testimony before unmasking the killer, usually in a one-on-one situation at the end.

Although the point at which Columbo realises who the killer is isn't revealed, the viewer always gets the impression that he knows almost from the beginning and then he uses his investigative skills to play cat-and-mouse with the suspect. In this way, each story was driven by the interaction of the principal characters through their dialogue rather than by action or elaborate set pieces.

The show won an Emmy in its first season and ran until 1978. When NBC pulled the plug, ABC revived it in 1989, where it remained until 2003, by which time 69 feature-length episodes had been broadcast. In 2007 Falk mentioned reprising the role but he was soon diagnosed with dementia and was unable to film a final case. His condition deteriorated quite rapidly and he died in 2011 at the age of 83.

Cracker

Cracker was a British crime drama set in Manchester that starred Robbie Coltrane as criminal psychologist Doctor Edward 'Fitz' Fitzgerald. It was conceived as a *Columbo*-style series by Jimmy McGovern, although the similarities between the two shows – revealing the killer at the beginning and having the unkempt and rather uncomfortable hero assigned to the case – were offset by Fitz's trouble bringing the right person to justice. Indeed in the *One Day a Lemming will Fly* episode police arrest the wrong man, and in *Men Should Weep* a serial rapist ends up killing his victim.

McGovern preferred this gritty approach because he wanted to emphasise the emotional and psychological aspects of police work rather than correct procedure, so the relationships between the characters were more credible than in shows such as *Prime Suspect*. He wrote the majority of the material himself, although Paul Abbott contributed heavily to the second series.

Fitz was a classic antihero: he drank, smoked, gambled and gave little thought to his shambolic appearance. He was, however, a brilliant psychologist with a big heart who was more determined than his colleagues to find the truth when it seemed some of them would settle for simply making arrests.

Coltrane was perfect for the role and it drew good audiences for the three series and 25 episodes. Despite its popularity, Coltrane refused to return unless McGovern agreed to write another series, which never materialised. He did, however, make a comeback for

the one-off special *Nine Eleven* in 2006, which saw Fitz investigating the murder of a nightclub comedian. The series was exported to America but audiences didn't relate to the storylines and only 16 episodes were aired.

Criminal Minds

Criminal Minds is an American drama following an FBI psychological profiling team as they try to identify criminals. The brainchild of Jeff Davis, it has starred, amongst others, Thomas Gibson as Aaron Hotchner, head of the behavioural analysis unit (BAU); Shemar Moore as Derek Morgan, a supervisory special agent; Andrea Cook as Special Agent Jennifer Jareau; Lola Glaudini as Elle Greenaway; and Mandy Patinkin as Senior Agent Jason Gideon, the BAU's best criminal profiler.

The show has been criticised by some reviewers as being overly complicated, and the application of several confusing conditions to a single person is unrealistic. Despite these unfavourable reviews, the performances of the cast have been universally praised and each series has drawn more than 12 million viewers per episode. Indeed in season two, *The Big Game* episode drew 26 million viewers. The show is now in its ninth year and has already been renewed for a 10th. So far, 207 episodes have been broadcast.

CSI

In the early 1990s writer Anthony Zuiker submitted a script to producer Jerry Bruckheimer in the hope of convincing him there was a series in the crime scene investigation concept. Bruckheimer liked the script and approached ABC, NBC, Fox and CBS, although only the latter showed any interest. Actor William Petersen was called in to play CSI Supervisor Gil Grissom in a pilot, and studio executives were so pleased with the result that they commissioned a series in 2000. It was to air on Friday evenings after *The Fugitive* but it soon claimed a larger audience share, which seemed to secure its future.

The show centres on the lives of crime scene investigators in Las Vegas as they examine the aftermath of a murder. Various people assist with the investigation, from blood experts to criminal psychologists,

forensic pathologists to toxicologists. It has attracted some criticism for the level of violence and sexual content for a primetime show, as well as for its unrealistic portrayal of police procedure. Real crime scene investigators, for example, don't then become involved in the detective work relating to the evidence they have collected, and they certainly don't conduct raids, pursue suspects and interrogate witnesses. Authorities have also criticised the show for giving the public a false impression of how crimes are solved and how quickly results can be achieved. Forensic analysis can take months, which clearly wouldn't work onscreen.

The level of criticism is perhaps indicative of how popular the show has become. *CSI* and its various spinoffs like *CSI: Miami* and *CSI: NY* are now

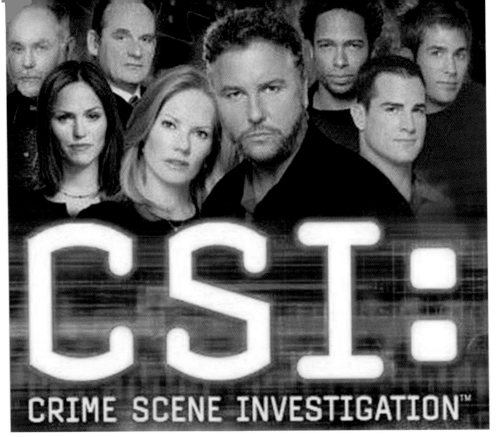

among the most-watched programs in the world, and between them they have won countless awards. In 2005 the Quentin Tarantino-directed season finale *Grave Danger* drew an American audience of 35 million, twice the number for any other show that evening. Having aired 315 episodes over 14 seasons, and with actors of the calibre of Ted Danson and Elisabeth Shue driving the series forward, *CSI* looks set to add to its 75 million viewers worldwide.

Dalziel & Pascoe

Originally based on the novels by Reginald Hill, *Dalziel & Pascoe* was a British television drama following the lives and cases of Detective Superintendent Andy Dalziel

– pronounced Dee-ell and played by Warren Clarke – and Detective Inspector Peter Pascoe, played by Colin Buchanan. It was set in Yorkshire and ran on the BBC from 1996 until 2007.

Although the buddy cop premise had been seen many times before, the two characters could hardly have been more different and they fell out at every available opportunity. The utterly insensitive and un-PC Dalziel was vulgar, loud and unhealthy but he had a good heart and doggedly pursued leads to get results. The mild-mannered Pascoe was college educated, polite and timid by comparison. Despite their different backgrounds, beliefs and methods, this unlikely duo combined to form a formidable crime-fighting unit. The series was axed in 2007 after 46 episodes.

Dempsey and Makepeace

Dempsey and Makepeace was created and produced by Ranald Graham for London Weekend Television. Having helped pen *The Sweeney* and *The Professionals*, Graham had excellent credentials and he brought a good-humoured but often gritty drama to the screen in 1985.

It featured the classic odd couple pairing of officers in the shape of brash working-class New Yorker Lieutenant James Dempsey (played by Michael Brandon) and British aristocrat Sergeant Harriet Makepeace, both of whom were assigned to an armed response unit of the Metropolitan Police.

Having seen his partner killed in a botched drugs raid, Dempsey discovered that corruption amongst New York's finest had reached epidemic levels. His position within the force compromised, he was sent to London to work alongside Lady Makepeace, daughter of Lord Winfield. Their wildly different backgrounds gave the writers plenty of scope to have fun at the characters' expense but they eventually bonded and formed a solid crime-fighting team.

The 'will they, won't they' aspect to the pair's relationship, which was blossoming in real life, provided both light relief and an extra layer of drama, and the show became an instant hit in the UK. It was sold throughout Europe, particularly in the Eastern Bloc, before being exported to America. It didn't fare as well across the pond and never achieved the same following it had in the UK. After two years, three series and 30 episodes, the show was culled by ITV in 1986.

DEMPSEY AND MAKEPEACE

Dixon of Dock Green

Dixon of Dock Green was the brainchild of writer Ted Willis, although he also maintained one hand on the production. The series was listed as a police drama but it was more light entertainment as it focused on everyday life at a London police station. The emphasis was on solving petty crime with solid police work and empathy with victims and villains rather than the more overtly aggressive style of shows like *Z-Cars*.

The series first aired in 1955, and it introduced a title character who was a father figure to colleagues and who ran the station as if they were family. Jack Warner's portrayal of Dixon as an old-school London 'bobby' was roundly praised. (Having cut his teeth as a radio comedian and then later in films, Warner was a household name and he brought a warmth and humanity to the part.) Dixon's wife had been killed during an air raid in the Second World War, leaving him to raise their daughter alone. A later episode mentioned his only son also being killed during the war, so the British public identified with him immediately.

The series ran for 432 episodes until 1976, by which time Warner was 80 and it was obvious to viewers that his policing days were over. It had been a phenomenal success, however, regularly attracting 13 million viewers, even during a period of stiff competition from *Z-Cars*. It's tragic that the BBC mislaid or wiped most of the original tapes for the series because only 32 complete episodes and parts of 19 others remain. Despite this, Dixon's catchphrase 'Evening, all' has forged a place in our lexicon, and in 2005 the series was revived on radio with David Calder in the title role. David Tennant added weight as Andy Crawford, while Charlie Brooks played Mary Dixon.

Dragnet

Dragnet is one of the foundations on which all radio and television crime dramas were built. The police procedural series was by then a popular genre but none carried the realism and authenticity of Jack Webb's creation. Indeed the word dragnet means apprehending criminals using a series of coordinated measures.

Webb was primarily an actor and he first came up with the premise while taking on the role of a forensic scientist in the 1948 film He Walked by Night, which was based on troubled veteran Erwin Walker's violent crime spree two years earlier.

Webb immersed himself in research, riding with LA cops on night patrols, learning all the jargon at the police academy and even studying the interior layout of the police department's headquarters. He then took the treatment to NBC but they initially rejected it as there were too many crime dramas on air. Webb refused to take no for an answer and eventually convinced NBC to give the radio show a short run. Sergeant Joe Friday had arrived.

The first few months were spent ironing out teething problems and allowing the characters to develop to the point where Dragnet had a following. Scripts were tightened up so the details and dialogue that helped police work translate to the medium became the focus. Webb insisted that plots reflected real life rather than the drama of Hollywood. While some episodes did cover violent crime, many centred on cheque fraud or shoplifting. For episodes featuring these rather mundane themes, the only way to keep listeners' interest was with quality scripts that kept the pace high.

The original radio show eventually ran from 1949 until 1957, but, after only three years, Webb's creation had sufficient credibility to make the leap to the small screen. Webb endeared himself to colleagues by insisting that the radio team should form the backbone of the television crew. The pilot aired in 1951 and it was so successful that it was commissioned early the following year.

Webb maintained his eye for detail and the interior of the Los Angeles police department was faithfully reproduced on screen. But the show began to feel a little dated towards the end of the 1950s and Webb voluntarily retired Joe Friday so he could concentrate on other projects. He revived the series in 1967 and it once again enjoyed good ratings, although Webb again pulled the plug after a fourth season in 1970. There were rumours of another comeback in 1982 but Webb died suddenly from a heart attack and the plan was shelved.

Dragnet remains an iconic police drama. It has spawned several films, numerous spinoffs and countless imitations and parodies. In all its guises, 762 episodes were eventually broadcast, with the latest incarnation winding down in 2004.

CHESTERFIELD'S DRAGNET—THURS. ON NBC TV, TUES. ON NBC RADIO

Due South

Due South was a Canadian crime drama set in Chicago. Creator Paul Haggis began his writing career on series like *The Love Boat* and *Diff'rent Strokes*, but he then moved onto *The Tracey Ullman Show* and *L.A. Law* (he would eventually write and produce *Million Dollar Baby* and *Crash*, both of which earned him Academy Awards).

Haggis pitched the idea of a Royal Canadian Mounted Policeman, Benton Fraser (played by Paul Gross), coming to Chicago from Toronto to search for his father's killer. CTV commissioned a television movie in 1994 and it was so successful when shown in the US on CBS that a continuing drama series was ordered.

Having teamed up with partner Ray Vecchio (David Marciano), Fraser and his trusty sidekick, a half-wolf called Diefenbaker, set about solving crime in the city. Fraser was a little stereotypical as the polite, truthful and determined Mountie, but his endearing character, unusual techniques (licking rubbish as part of the investigative process) and easy charm carried a harmless and entertaining series. His dog was also one of the ingredients that made the series work. Dief was extremely loyal to Fraser and helped the Mountie escape from countless scrapes, although while in the US he developed a taste for junk food.

Such was its initial popularity that a number of high-profile stars – Leslie Nielsen, Mark Ruffalo and Rick Rossovich – appeared in later episodes. It was the first Canadian drama to have a primetime slot on American television but CBS cancelled the series after the first season. It remained popular in

Canada and the UK, however, which allowed the production company to fund a second season (this was then shown on CBS). With more funding from abroad, the series was able to run for 67 episodes until 1999, and it regularly attracted eight million viewers in the UK.

The First 48

The First 48 is an American documentary series following real homicide investigators as they are assigned to cases. The program often follows the investigation until its conclusion but it concentrates on the first 48 hours. It gives valuable insight into the methods used by crime scene investigators to collect forensic evidence, as well as the skills employed by detectives to interview witnesses and identify potential suspects.

It first aired in 2004, and by 2009 it was drawing up to 2.5 million viewers and had become the most popular non-fiction police series on American television. Follow-up shows examined the trials of those captured, while other spinoffs tried to trace missing persons or deal with interviewing those convicted of the crimes.

The series remains popular but it hasn't been without controversy. Witnesses do not have their identities concealed, for example, so they could potentially be targeted by criminals or their associates looking for revenge. The show also has virtually unrestricted access to police files, a privilege not granted to local media.

In 2009 Taiwan Smart was charged with the murders of his two roommates. His story was featured on *The First 48* but police bungled the investigation and the program misrepresented key witness statements. Smart was released and has since mounted a campaign to sue the city of Miami for false imprisonment.

Then, in 2010, a seven-year-old girl, Aiyana Jones, was shot and killed during a raid by a Detroit SWAT team that was being filmed for the show. The officer responsible, Joseph Weekley, was

THE FIRST [48]
MISSING PERSONS

charged with involuntary manslaughter and reckless endangerment with a gun but the jury couldn't reach a verdict.

Producers at the show have repeatedly refused permission for the tape of the incident to be viewed.

Foyle's War

Foyle's War was created by Anthony Horowitz, best known for his Alex Rider spy novels that chronicled the life of a 14-year-old recruited to MI6. The series is set in Hastings during and just after the Second World War and Horowitz went to great lengths to ensure historical accuracy both with the script and the locations.

Detective Chief Superintendent (one of the minor factual inaccuracies as this rank wasn't introduced by the Metropolitan Police until 1949) Christopher Foyle, played by Michael Kitchen, investigates opportunist crimes whereby the perpetrators have used the confusion of war to cover their tracks. He is ably assisted by Detective Sergeant Paul Milner (Anthony Howell) and his driver Samantha Stewart (Honeysuckle Weeks).

There are superficial echoes of *Columbo* in that Foyle is quiet, methodical and brutally honest, and his adversaries frequently underestimate him. Foyle is a widower, however, who repeatedly locks horns with the military and intelligence services when investigating black-market business deals and occasionally murder.

Foyle is the son of a policeman who isn't ashamed to admit that he was forced to kill while fighting at Passchendaele in the Great War. Although he hated being enlisted in the army, he repeatedly requests a transfer to the war department during the series. He eventually accepts that detective work will dominate his civilian life, although he likes to relax by fishing (well) and playing golf (badly). He later eschews civilian life by joining MI5, while Samantha becomes his junior clerk.

First broadcast in 2002, the 90-minute episodes usually stand alone, although

subplots do continue throughout each series. Ratings remained high throughout the first five seasons so it came as something of a shock when ITV Director of Programming Simon Shaps called time on *Foyle's War* in 2007. Horowitz shelved several scripts set in 1943 and '44 but then ITV recanted their decision and the latest series began filming in early 2014.

The Fugitive

The Fugitive was an American drama that took the traditional cop show in a different direction because it was seen from the suspect's point of view. Creator Roy Huggins had written three novels in the 1940s, and, when Columbia Pictures bought the rights to *The Double Take* in 1948, he was signed up to adapt the book for the big screen. Having graduated into the movies, he also worked as a TV producer for Warner Brothers and ABC, for whom he penned *Maverick*, *77 Sunset Strip* and then *The Fugitive*.

The series lasted for four seasons and 120 episodes between 1963 and 1967. The premise was that Doctor Richard Kimble (played by David Janssen) was convicted of murdering his wife but, while he was on the way to prison and death row, his train derailed and allowed him to escape. The second hook was that Kimble was in fact wrongly convicted of the murder. He'd seen a one-armed man escaping the scene so it became his compulsion to catch the real killer before he was apprehended by Lieutenant Philip Gerard (Barry Morse).

Kimble was a respected paediatrician but he and his wife had been arguing about adopting children after she was left infertile after an operation to save her life during a failed pregnancy. He went out for a drive to cool off and almost ran over the one-armed man fleeing his house when he returned. Kimble found Helen dead inside but, as neighbours had only heard them arguing and didn't know Richard had left the house, he was convicted of the murder and sentenced to death. Having escaped, the intelligent and resourceful Kimble used his skills to blend in among the locals of several small towns while he searched for the one-armed man.

Gerard, on the other hand, cared little for Kimble's predicament as his personal opinion about his innocence or guilt was inconsequential. In the eyes of the law Kimble was guilty, and Gerard pursued him relentlessly so that the law could be upheld. By the fourth season, however, Gerard was having doubts about the validity of the conviction. The two met several times during the series and the tension between the pair was captured beautifully on screen.

The second part of the final episode, in which Gerard, Kimble and the one-armed man finally faced-off, was watched by approximately 80 million Americans, a record that stood for 13 years until the *Who Done It* episode of Dallas aired in 1980. The show spawned many variants and spinoffs but the most successful was the 1993 film of the same name starring Harrison Ford as Kimble and Tommy Lee Jones as Gerard, the latter winning an Academy Award for Best Supporting Actor.

Hawaii Five-O

Hawaii Five-O was created by screenwriter and producer Leonard Freeman for CBS in 1968. He had moved to Hawaii after suffering a heart attack, so the idea for the show was likely borne from a conversation with Governor John Burns. Richard Boone, Gregory Peck and Robert Browne were all considered for the role of Detective Lieutenant Steve McGarrett but the part went to Jack Lord at the last minute and he flew to Hawaii two days later.

Hawaii wasn't ideally suited for producing a major television series but Lord was a tough taskmaster and he worked a crew that was essentially learning on the job extremely hard. His perseverance paid off and production soon moved from a dilapidated Quonset Hut in Pearl City to Fort Ruger, and then to a purpose-built studio in Diamond Head. Production was almost exclusively limited to the islands, although a few episodes were filmed in Los Angeles, Hong Kong and Singapore.

McGarrett was a former naval officer whose team headed up a fictional state police force. He and sidekick Danny 'Danno' Williams (James MacArthur) came up against a variety of criminals from foreign spies to murderers, drug runners and international crime syndicates. At the end of each episode, and with the suspect in their custody, McGarrett would invariably bark the instruction to Williams: "Book 'em, Danno!" before occasionally adding the charge, such as "murder one".

The series focused on the cases and rarely explored the characters' backgrounds, although it was clear that McGarrett, much like Joe Friday in

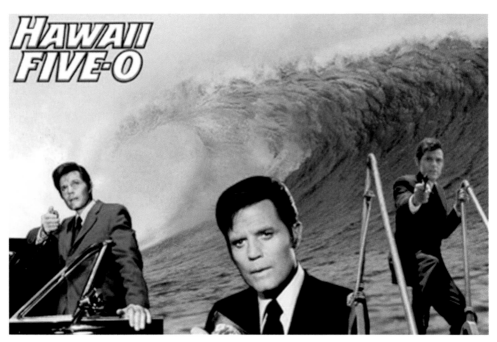

Dragnet, was a cop married to his job.

Hawaii Five-O was the longest-running crime series on US television until 2003 when *Law & Order* ran into its 13th year. Reza Badiyi's opening credits and Morton Stevens's theme music (performed by The Ventures) remain iconic, and in 2010 the sequence was voted the fourth best opening to a show in television history. Although the series was discontinued in 1980 after 284 episodes had been broadcast, a revamp was scheduled for 1997. The pilot wasn't picked up by any of the networks, however, although the Five-0 did make a comeback with a new series in 2010. The latest incarnation is now in its fourth season having aired 90 episodes.

Heartbeat

Heartbeat was a British police drama set in 1960s' Yorkshire and loosely based on the *Constable* series of books by Peter Walker. The title derived from the medical themes of the plots and the traditional bobby's beat. It was written primarily for its first star, Nick Berry, but many actors have appeared as the lead over the years. It centred on the police station in the fictional hamlet of Ashfordly, in particular the new man in town, PC Nick Rowan, who had just arrived from London.

It managed to avoid most of the 'swinging sixties' clichés, although references were made to pop culture, hippies and psychedelia. Instead, it had a powerful musical soundtrack from the era, with Berry himself singing the Buddy Holly-penned theme tune (his version reached number two in the UK singles chart in 1992).

The first series focused exclusively on Rowan and his wife Kate (Niamh Cusack), a local doctor. PC Rowan's arrival in the village caused a stir amongst the locals but his easygoing nature saw him gain first acceptance, then respect and finally admiration. Kate had been born in Yorkshire so was familiar with the area but she too found it difficult to connect initially, due in part to the locals finding it hard to accept a female doctor. She ended up running the village practice however, although she then fell pregnant, which caused marital problems. Although the couple grew to rejoice in the pregnancy, Kate was diagnosed with leukaemia (which she kept to herself) and died shortly after giving birth. It would take Rowan two years to overcome his grief but he did later re-marry.

The series was incredibly popular in the UK and around the world. It regularly attracted 15 million viewers and won programme of the year twice. When Nick Berry left after 98 episodes in 1998, many feared the show would fold, but by then it had an ensemble cast and the writers easily switched the attention between them to create new storylines.

However, by 2009 the show's audience had fallen to around six million and cast and crew were summoned to a meeting to discuss the future. ITV eventually decided to cancel the show, and, although rumours abounded that Sky might buy them out and continue production, it finally wound down after 18 series and 372 episodes.

Hill Street Blues

Hill Street Blues was created by Steven Bochco (*L.A. Law*, *Doogie Howser, M.D.* and *NYPD Blue*) and Michael Kozoll, and it remains one of the most important police procedural dramas in television history. NBC appointed MTM Enterprises to develop the series so Bochco and Kozoll were invited to write the initial episodes.

The pair were given creative freedom so they introduced a number of ideas that have since become the norm for television dramas: the episodes incorporated plots that continued into subsequent shows; tension was increased by showing the conflict between the characters' work and private lives; and real issues were addressed using contemporary language. Innovative filming techniques were also used, such as employing handheld cameras and cutting quickly between stories to give the show a documentary feel.

The writers also avoided saying where the series was set, although parts of the action clearly took place in the northeast of the country around New York, Chicago and Boston. The series chronicled the lives of officers from a single urban police station, and it broke new ground by giving lead roles to African/American and Hispanic actors.

The pilot aired in 1981 and, although it was popular, the show took several seasons to find its niche and become must-see television alongside *Fame*, *Taxi* and *Cheers*. The original cast boasted the likes of Daniel Travanti as Captain Frank Furillo; Veronica Hamel as Joyce Davenport; Michael Conrad as Sergeant Phil Esterhaus; and Bruce Weitz as Detective Mick Belker.

Despite ranking poorly on the Nielsen ratings, *Hill Street Blues* soon hit its straps and, in seven seasons and 146 episodes, the show earned an incredible 98 Emmy Award nominations. In 1993, six years after it had ended, *TV Guide* voted it the best cop show and best drama in 40 years of television. It remains a seminal police procedural that has often been copied but never equalled.

Inspector
George Gently

Inspector George Gently is a British crime drama based on the *George Gently* novels by Alan Hunter. Martin Shaw (*The Professionals*, *Judge John Deed*) plays the title role, although he is ably assisted by Detective Sergeant John Bacchus (Lee Ingleby), WPC Rachel Coles (Lisa

McGrillis) and Police Constable Taylor (Simon Hubbard). The books were set in Norfolk but the series transferred the action to County Durham and Northumberland.

The pilot was broadcast in 2007 to good reviews. Inspector Gently's wife was murdered by a local criminal, which forces the officer to delay his retirement. Each episode thereafter stood alone, with a separate case drawn from the novels solved every week. Series six aired in 2014, although as production costs are high and the running times are long (most shows are feature length), only 19 episodes have been produced so far.

The show has proved extremely popular in the UK and abroad, and it is now shown in countries from Argentina to Australia, Canada to Denmark, and Slovenia to Sweden and the United States.

Inspector Morse

Inspector Morse was based on the novels by Colin Dexter and adapted for the screen by Tony Warren, who is best known for creating *Coronation Street*. Morse was unlike the previous generation of detectives such as Poirot and Sherlock Holmes because, although blessed with brilliant insight, keen observation and great powers of deduction, he wasn't always right.

Despite him often arresting the wrong man or making incorrect assumptions and drawing inaccurate conclusions, Morse's talents were clearly wasted in rural Oxfordshire, but his lack of ambition and conflicts with superiors conspired to deny him promotion. In these respects, Morse is much more identifiable than the classic hero or even antihero. He drinks heavily, flirts outrageously (with little success) and stumbles through a life crammed with uneasy personal relationships. (His ambivalence towards his own health finally reaches a head when he succumbs to a drink-related heart attack.)

Morse also likes orchestral music, poetry, ale and classic cars – his red 1960 Mark 2 Jaguar became as recognisable as the character, and by 2005 it was worth more than £100,000.

John Thaw was an inspired choice to play the lead. He'd previously acted on stage alongside Sir Laurence Olivier and he then appeared as a detective with an aversion to alcohol in several episodes of the police drama *Z-Cars*. This was perfect grounding to play Jack Regan in *The Sweeney*, which catapulted Thaw into the big league and established him as a major star.

The brash and hardnosed Regan was the polar opposite of the softly spoken and

well-educated Morse, but Thaw seemed to become both characters with effortless ease. Indeed it's difficult to imagine anyone else playing the curmudgeonly crossword-addicted pedant. Thaw's interaction with downtrodden sidekick Detective Sergeant Lewis (Kevin Whately) ensured both men became cult heroes and was the main reason why 18 million people tuned in every week to watch the two try to solve yet another murder.

The series ran for 33 feature-length episodes from 1987 to 1993, although the cast reunited for another five specials between 1995 and 2000. Thaw died at the age of 60 in 2002, so, as a mark of respect, a series featuring Lewis didn't appear until 2006. In 2012 a prequel called Endeavour (Morse's first name) aired in the UK. Its second series was broadcast in early 2014.

Ironside

Ironside was created by Collier Young, a writer who also produced *The Hitch-Hiker* and *The Wild, Wild West*. The show centred on former San Francisco detective Robert Ironside (played by Raymond Burr), a veteran police officer who was left paralysed from the waist down after being shot by a sniper. As he was wheelchair-bound and unable to compete physically with potential criminals, the show's hook was that Ironside had to rely on his wits to solve cases and bring them to justice.

Burr began his career on Broadway and radio, although he usually played the villain. He then collected two Emmys (1959, 1961) for his portrayal of Perry Mason, a fictional defence lawyer, in a series that ran from 1957 until 1966. Burr then defected from CBS to Universal to play *Ironside*, which eventually aired on NBC from 1967 to 1975 and ran to 199 episodes. He would receive another six Emmy and two Golden Globe nominations for the role.

Filmed in Los Angeles, the show only became a modest hit but that didn't stop stars of the calibre of Harrison Ford, David Cassidy, Jack Lord, Jodie Foster, Bruce Lee and Burgess Meredith appearing as guests. The main cast reunited in 1993 for a TV movie special and, 20 years later, Blair Underwood starred in the title role in a remake that only lasted four episodes.

Juliet Bravo

Juliet Bravo was a British television series that ran for 88 episodes between 1980 and 1985. It was created by Ian Kennedy Martin, whose other credits included *The Sweeney* and the 1975 action film *Mitchell*, and it was set in the fictional town of Hartley in Lancashire. Although many viewers initially thought the title of the show was also the name of the female lead, it was actually her radio call sign J-B, which in the NATO phonetic alphabet corresponds to Juliet Bravo.

The police crime drama had been established in the 1950s with the likes of *Dixon of Dock Green*, and *Juliet Bravo* was released in direct competition with ITV's *The Gentle Touch*. Both series saw the introduction of female leads who not only had to fight crime but also contend with prejudice and sexism from male officers.

Stephanie Turner had played Dennis Waterman's on-screen spouse in *The Sweeney* and WPC Howarth in *Z-Cars* so she was a natural choice to play Inspector Jean Darblay in *Juliet Bravo*. Turner left the show after three series however, so producers promoted Inspector Kate Longton to the lead role (played by Anna Carteret). Carteret was an established star having appeared in *The Saint* and she would go on to greater things with *Peak Practice* and *Holby City*.

Kojak

Kojak's origins can be traced to the book *Justice in the Back Room* by Selwyn Raab. The book dealt with themes of prejudice and civil rights, which gave Academy Award-winning writer Abby Mann plenty of ammunition for plots centred on the 11th Precinct of the New York Police Department. Indeed this gritty urban drama was a far cry from the softer procedural dramas of the late 1960s.

Lieutenant Theodore Kojak (played by Telly Savalas) was stubborn and methodical, but he was also prepared to bend the rules if it meant making an arrest or securing a conviction. In early episodes he was a smoker, but by 1971 tobacco advertising was banned from US television so the character, as well as Savalas himself, turned to sucking lollipops as a substitute. The Tootsie Pop eventually became one of the most recognisable props in the show, although neither Savalas nor the character actually managed to quit smoking.

The series attracted an immediate following and guest stars included Maud Adams, Richard Gere, Paul Anka, Harvey Keitel, Sylvester Stallone and Christopher Walken. (Telly's younger brother George played Sergeant Heathcliff 'Fatso' Stavros.) The series also made a huge impact on popular culture around the world: in Brazil in the 1970s bald men became known as Kojaks, and the phrase "I wouldn't give a chance to Kojak" (meaning I'd better not leave any clue, or I'd better not let anyone see my mistake) entered the lexicon; in Chile the word Kojak became slang for lollipop; and because the character usually drew his gun from his front right pocket as

he approached a potentially dangerous situation, this became known in the US as drawing Kojak style.

Due to declining ratings the show was cancelled in 1978 after five seasons and 118 episodes, although reruns were hugely successful and Savalas was eventually persuaded to return for two TV movies, *The Belarus File* (1985) and *The Price of Justice* (1987). Two years later ABC aired five two-hour specials. Ving Rhames then slipped into Kojak's shoes for a season in 2005, and there are rumours of a Vin Diesel film in the near future.

Law & Order

Law & Order is one of the most popular and long-running shows in the history of American television. Creator Dick Wolf originally wrote for *Hill Street Blues* (for which he received an Emmy nomination) before producing the *Miami Vice* series that ran from 1984–1989. In 1990 he proposed *Law & Order*, a series that focused on aspects of the criminal justice system, to NBC. As of 2014, the show in all its various guises has aired 1025 episodes.

The initial series ran for 20 seasons and 456 episodes, with the first half of each show focusing on the forensic investigation of a crime. The second half of each episode then moved to the district attorney's office in New York to examine the case for the prosecution. The show was discontinued in 2010, although Wolf tried (unsuccessfully) to revive it on cable television.

There were, however, several franchises already in place: in 1999 *Law & Order: Special Victims Unit* was created to examine sexually motivated crime and offences involving children. It has now aired 339 episodes in 15 seasons. *Law & Order: Criminal Intent* ran from 2001 until 2011, with 195 episodes being broadcast. It focused on the lives of the criminals rather than the pursuing officers, thereby trying to justify their motivation for committing what were usually high-profile crimes.

Law & Order: Trial by Jury only lasted for a single season (2005-06). It followed the legal teams as they prepared their cases before going to trial. It was cancelled after just 13 episodes due to poor ratings. *Law & Order: LA* also only lasted for one season. It was the first franchise to be based outside

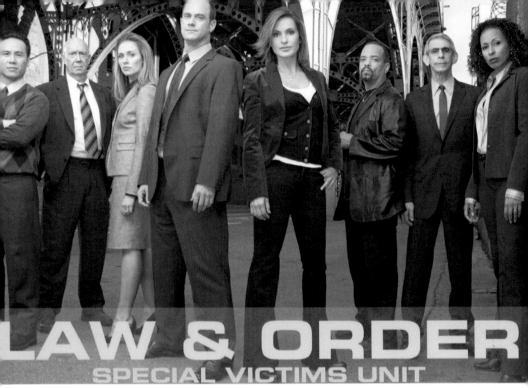

LAW & ORDER
SPECIAL VICTIMS UNIT

New York and, with a similar format to the original series, it was expected to do well. Poor reviews and low ratings forced NBC to pull the plug, however.

Overall, the franchise has been extremely successful: a TV film was released in 1998, and the show also spawned several video games whereby players investigated crimes, interviewed witnesses and then prosecuted the cases. Many other series are based in the same universe as the franchise, such as *Homicide: Life on the Street*, *New York Undercover*, *Deadline*, *Conviction*, *In Plain Sight* and *Chicago PD*. The show also has spinoffs in countries around the world, notably *Law & Order: UK*, which was first broadcast in 2009; and two versions set in Moscow.

Magnum, P.I.

*M*agnum was a crime drama from the pens of Donald Bellisario and Glen Larson, whose credits also included *Airwolf*, *Quantum Leap*, *JAG* and *NCIS*. It followed the exploits of Thomas Magnum (played by Tom Selleck), a former naval officer and SEAL Team sniper who served with distinction in the Vietnam War. His final posting was with the Office of Naval Intelligence, although he resigned after 10 years having become disillusioned with military life. He then embarked on a career as a private investigator on the Hawaiian island of Oahu.

The series was set around Robin's Nest, the fictional beachfront estate of mysterious and always-absent novelist Robin Masters. As the writer was never home, he entrusted the caretaking role to Jonathan Higgins and the security arrangements to Magnum. To keep himself busy, Magnum took on cases that suited him, all the while knowing he could count on help from Theo 'TC' Calvin who ran a helicopter charter service, and Rick Wright who owned the local bar. In many ways, Magnum seemed to have the perfect lifestyle: he lived in a luxury beach-house, drove Masters's red Ferrari 308 (one of the most iconic screen cars of all time), and was usually surrounded by a bevy of beautiful women.

The series essentially took over from Hawaii Five-0 and was an instant hit. Stars like Ted Danson, Ernest Borgnine, Frank Sinatra and Sharon Stone all made guest appearances. Selleck himself famously missed out on playing Indiana Jones in the first Spielberg film of the series (*Raiders of the Lost Ark*) because he had just signed a contract tying him to

Magnum, which was ready to shoot in the first few months of 1980. The part of Indy went to Harrison Ford, although it then transpired that a writers' strike delayed production on *Magnum* so Selleck would have been able to play the archaeological adventurer.

Magnum ran for eight seasons and 162 episodes on CBS before being axed in 1988. In their time on the show, both Selleck and John Hillerman (Higgins) won Emmys, while Bellisario and Larson received an Edgar Award for the Best Episode in a TV series.

Miami Vice

Miami Vice broke new ground in the 1980s and has since become one of the most recognisable and influential police dramas in television history. Two theories have emerged about its conception, the first being that Brandon Tartikoff (head of entertainment at NBC) wrote a memo asking for ideas for an MTV cop show, and the second being that *Hill Street Blues* writer Anthony Yerkovich came up with the concept after hearing about vice cops confiscating property from drug dealers.

What isn't disputed is that Yerkovich penned a two-hour pilot based in South Florida about a pair of vice cops combating drug smuggling and prostitution. The production team realised that they had to appeal to the MTV generation so they used high-octane rock and pop music – particularly the pounding keyboards of Jan Hammer who wrote the theme tune – and groundbreaking visual effects to drive the action. Hammer's score won two Grammy Awards and was later voted the best theme tune of all time.

NBC realised they too could contribute to the aural experience so they decided to broadcast the show in stereo. Indeed the soundtrack became such a key part of the series that artists queued up to have their songs played, while the rest – Phil Collins, Glenn Frey, Frank Zappa, Sheena Easton et al – simply had to make do with guest appearances.

Yerkovich knew he could draw upon the diverse cultures and socioeconomic groups in Florida to add realism and credibility to the series. The drug trade, for example, directly influenced the service trade so there was always a chain of evidence and a trail of money for the

cops to follow. If there was one criticism, it was that almost every episode ended in a violent shootout that usually claimed the lives of criminals who should have been brought to justice in front of a jury, but the 1980s was the time of films like *Cobra*, *Beverley Hills Cop*, *Rambo* and *Commando* and audiences loved the explosive ending.

Several major film stars – Nick Nolte, Mickey Rourke – were considered for the role of James 'Sonny' Crockett but 30 years ago it simply wasn't economical for Hollywood actors to tackle TV work so the part eventually went to Don Johnson. Philip Michael Thomas was then chosen to play Ricardo 'Rico' Tubbs. The pair went through so many outfits in each episode that the show ended up influencing men's fashion worldwide. The show even popularised brands of firearm (Bren Ten and Smith & Wesson), sports car (Ferrari 365 GTS/4 Spyder and Testarossa) and boat (Scarab 38KV).

Miami Vice ran for five seasons and 111 episodes between 1985 and 1989. It was axed only after schedulers unwisely pitted it against *Dallas* and then wondered why the ratings fell, although by then the series was tired and formulaic and failed to reinvent itself.

Midsomer Murders

Midsomer Murders is a British crime drama based on the *Chief Inspector Barnaby* books by Caroline Graham. In the initial run, Anthony Horowitz adapted the books for the screen and John Nettles was chosen to play DCI Tom Barnaby. The series is set in the town of Causton in the fictional county of Midsomer. For such a peaceful area it has an extremely high crime rate, with nearly 100 murders investigated to date. This allows the writers and cast to bring a darkly comic slant to much of the action.

Nettles's previous characters included Jim Bergerac and Giles Sutton from *Heartbeat* so he was perfect for the role. The pilot aired in 1997 and viewing figures soon stabilised at around six million. In 2009, however, Nettles announced that he would be leaving the show after two more seasons. Fears that the program would falter without its lead were allayed when Neil Dudgeon took over as Detective Chief Inspector John Barnaby, Tom's younger cousin.

Midsomer Murders has been a huge hit worldwide, with countries from Australia, Bulgaria, Croatia, Iceland, India, Latvia, Serbia, South Korea and Ukraine all giving it a weekly slot in the scheduling. The show has attracted some controversy, however: in 2011 producer Brian True-May was suspended for claiming that the lack of racial diversity was because the series was a bastion of Englishness. While his comments were perhaps ill judged, it's difficult to argue with the fact that the ethnic population of small West Country towns is almost non-existent. True-May eventually apologised and he was reinstated, although he stepped down anyway before series 15.

Moonlighting

Moonlighting was proposed by ABC executive Lewis Erlicht and created by Glenn Caron. Erlicht liked Caron's work on *Taxi* and *Remington Steele* but he wanted the new detective show to be equal parts humour and drama. He also stipulated that it needed a major star and a newcomer, and that the pair had to interact in dramatic, comedic and romantic situations. The writers were also given free rein to experiment with the characters addressing the audience or referencing the network and its other shows, or even having the film crew unexpectedly pop into shot to play minor roles.

Caron was also given a big hand in the production side because *Moonlighting* was owned and produced in-house by ABC. This allowed the network to plough the show's profits into the production of future episodes. With a big budget at his disposal – two million dollars a show was double that of comparable dramas – Caron and director of photography Gerald Finnerman shot the show as if it was a movie, and the results spoke for themselves: the black-and-white episode *The Dream Sequence Always Rings Twice* earned an Emmy nomination.

The show starred Cybill Shepherd as Maddie Hayes, a former model who was left bankrupt by a crooked accountant. She formed a detective agency to make ends meet, using her status to attract clients. Bruce Willis played David Addison, a fast-talking detective with a rival agency who managed to convince Maddie that they'd be better off working together. It was a miracle that the on-screen chemistry worked so well because the actors often didn't get

along and there were frequent delays to shooting.

The series was a huge hit with audiences however, and it garnered 16 Emmy nominations in only its second year. Its decline is often linked with the consummation of the relationship between Maddie and David, but by then Shepherd was a mother and Willis was considering a switch to movies after the success of *Die Hard*. In 1989, after five seasons and 66 episodes, ABC cancelled the show due to falling ratings and production difficulties.

NCIS

NCIS (Naval Criminal Investigative Service) is another procedural drama from the creative team of Donald Bellisario and Don McGill. The series focuses on criminal investigations involving the American navy and Marine Corps, with both the concept and some of the characters being introduced in the CBS series *JAG*.

Agents from the fictional Major Case Response Team (MCRT) in Washington investigate high-profile cases, such as terrorist plots, kidnappings and murders on US naval bases. The team is headed by Special Agent Leroy Gibbs (played by Mark Harmon), and he is ably assisted by Senior Field Agent Tony DiNozzo (Michael Weatherly) and NSA analyst Eleanor Bishop (Emily Wickersham). Female interest had previously included Mossad Liaison Officer Ziva David (Cote de Pablo) and Abby Sciuto (Pauley Perrette).

Gibbs was a sniper with the marines but, when his first wife and child were killed by a Mexican drug baron, he joined the NCIS to track him down and avenge their deaths. He was eventually promoted to agent in charge of the MCRT, and he occasionally stands in as director of the NCIS. Tony DiNozzo was formerly a police detective who joined NCIS in 2001 after exposing corruption within the Baltimore PD. When the two previous female leads left the show, the character of Eleanor Bishop was written to replace them. She was poached from the NSA by the NCIS having agreed to a permanent move after helping the MCRT with a case.

The show was a moderate success in its first two years and attracted up to 14

NCIS
Naval Criminal Investigative Service

million viewers. By 2009 it reached the top spot for a scripted show and two years later it was drawing an audience of more than 20 million. In its 10th season (2012), it finally overtook *American Idol* and *Sunday Night Football* as the most watched show on American television.

It has become such a juggernaut that there are TV movies, several spinoffs (particularly *NCIS: Los Angeles*, starring Chris O'Donnell and LLCool J) and an official two-disc soundtrack. It is now into its 11th season and 255 episodes have been aired.

NYPD Blue

NYPD Blue was an American police procedural drama that followed the professional and personal lives of detectives from the fictional 15th Precinct in Manhattan. The series was created by Steven Bochco (*Hill Street Blues*, *L.A. Law*) and David Milch (*Brooklyn South*, *Deadwood*). It was an instant hit and ran for 261 episodes between 1993 and 2005.

The show was written for the character of John Kelly (David Caruso), with most of the series-one action revolving around his private life, but, with his departure at the end of the first season, the show moved to an ensemble format with the focus shifting slightly towards Sergeant Andy Sipowicz (Dennis Franz), Detective Diane Russell (Kim Delaney), Detective Bobby Simone (Jimmy Smits), Detective Danny Sorenson (Rick Schroder), and Detective John Clark (Mark-Paul Gosselaar).

Sipowicz was an alcoholic with behavioural issues who frequently angered partner Kelly, although respect and affection did eventually prevail. With Caruso's departure, the writers felt that Franz's character would have to sober up to keep his job, and he became the unofficial lead in the series thereafter.

The show was criticised by some for its excessive nudity, and the American Family Association even took out ads in newspapers calling for it to be boycotted. Although good ratings silenced most critics, the strength of the language and graphic violence also drew condemnation. More off-screen problems revolved around Milch's alcoholism and addictive personality, and he would often infuriate cast and

crew with last-minute set or script changes. Despite this, he was nominated for 13 Emmys, of which he won three.

The show as a whole was equally successful and regularly drew audiences of 15 million, but by 2003 viewing figures had fallen to below 10 million and the series was axed in 2005.

Perry Mason

Although the character of Perry Mason was a defence attorney, the dramatised court show was heavily influenced by police procedure and many of the supporting cast were detectives. Raymond Burr was chosen to play Mason (the character had first appeared in the books of Erle Stanley Gardner and many of the episodes were based on Gardner's stories) and the first half of each show dealt with how Burr's client interacted with the homicide victim. The second half then analysed the crime in the courtroom setting, with Mason working to establish his client's innocence, usually by proving the guilt of another character.

Gardner had seen *Perry Mason* adapted for the big screen in the 1930s but the films had been disappointing so he established Paisano Productions to look after his interests should any series be commissioned in the future. In 1957 he decided to produce a series, but William Hopper was originally considered for the title role while Raymond Burr was chosen to play DA Hamilton Burger. Burr eventually managed to convince Gardner that he would be a better Mason and the author agreed.

All but one of the shows was shot in black and white on location in Los Angeles. It was extremely popular and attracted guest stars of the calibre of Robert Redford, James Coburn, Burt Reynolds, Leonard Nimoy, Bette Davis and Fay Wray. Mason was extremely successful and only lost three cases of more than 300, one of which was overturned on appeal, although he did lose a civil case having been framed for witness tampering. This verdict was also

overturned.

The original series ran for nine seasons and 271 episodes before being discontinued in 1966. *The New Perry Mason* tried to revive interest in the character in 1973 but it was unsuccessful, although 30 TV movies that aired between 1985 and 1995 (with Burr back in the title role for the first 26 – he died in 1993) were well received.

Poirot

Although Agatha Christie's Belgian detective Hercule Poirot had been portrayed on radio and screen many times – notably by Albert Finney, Sir Peter Ustinov and Sir Ian Holm – David Suchet's interpretation for ITV in the UK is perhaps the best known and most faithful to the character in the books. Indeed Poirot was one of the most enduring characters of Christie's novels: he appeared in 33, as well as 50 short stories and a play (*Black Coffee*) between 1920 (*The Mysterious Affair at Styles*) and 1975 (*Curtain*). Christie was certainly influenced by the works of Sir Arthur Conan Doyle, and Poirot bears a strong resemblance to Alfred Mason's French Inspector Hanaud who appeared in the novel *At the Villa Rose* in 1910.

Clive Exton and Brian Eastman wrote and produced the first eight series of *Agatha Christie's Poirot*, after which Michele Buck and Damien Timmer were drafted in to revamp the series. Their influence led to the show dropping much of the subtle humour because the later novels were more psychologically driven. Several other writers have also contributed to the series, including Anthony Horowitz, Nick Dear and Ian Hallard.

Christie's family had seen Suchet's portrayal of Blott in Tom Sharpe's *Blott on the Landscape* and they were keen for him to take the role. Suchet agreed and immersed himself in the character to the point of obsession. He read every story in which Poirot appeared and wrote out all of the defining characteristics given him by the novelist. In this way he was almost able to become Poirot – right down to the quirks and irritating mannerisms

– before the first episode was filmed. Despite rumours that the show would be cancelled before Suchet had starred in every story in the canon (which was his ambition), the last few books were adapted into five episodes that aired in 2013.

The series helped launch the careers of a number of future stars: Joely Richardson appeared in *The Dream* (1989), Samantha Bond starred in *The Adventure of the Cheap Flat* (1990), and Christopher Eccleston had a part in *One, Two, Buckle My Shoe* (1992). Damian Lewis, Emily Blunt and Michael Fassbender also took on roles.

Agatha Christie's family, especially daughter Rosalind Hicks and grandson Mathew, reacted extremely positively to Suchet's portrayal of the detective. Praise from critics was almost universal, and *Poirot* received 20 BAFTA nominations for the first three series alone. In all, 13 series and 70 episodes aired between 1989 and 2013.

Police Camera Action!

Police Camera Action! introduced a compilation of videos shot from police cars in the line of duty. The ITV reality show was presented by Alastair Stewart from 1994 until 2002, by which time he'd been convicted twice for drink driving. The second time he lost control of his car while three times the drink-drive limit and crashed into a telegraph pole, which meant some episodes weren't shown for three years.

The in-car footage was often supplemented by media footage of bad driving, road crime and high-speed police pursuits in much the same way as the American shows *World's Wildest Police Videos* and *World's Scariest Police Chases*. (Almost every crime or pursuit was resolved in favour of the police, although some criminals did escape.)

In 2007 Stewart was joined by Adrian Simpson, with the latter reporting from locations around the country and providing voice overs to let the audience know how the chase was resolved if it didn't appear on camera. A final series – the sixth – presented by Gethin Jones aired in 2010 and took the number of episodes shown to 95, although the genre lives on in variants like *Police Stop!*, *Road Wars*, *Traffic Cops* (*Motorway Cops*), *Brit Cops* and *Street Crime UK*.

Police Squad!

Although only six episodes of *Police Squad!* aired in 1982, it remains a cult classic and spawned the hugely successful *The Naked Gun* film series. Having already written *Airplane!*, which spoofed the disaster movies that were being churned out by Hollywood in the late 1970s, Jim Abrahams, David Zucker and Jerry Zucker wanted to write a comedy that parodied the traditional police procedural.

Leslie Nielsen had impressed the writers with his performance in *Airplane!* so he was chosen to play lead character Detective Lieutenant Frank Drebin (a name plucked at random from a phone book). Alan North played Captain Ed Hocken, Ed Williams had a role as forensic scientist Ted Olson and Peter Lupus co-starred as Officer Norberg. 'Tiny Ron' Taylor, a seven-foot basketball player appeared as Big Al, although he was so tall his face was never shown. A host of famous special guest stars, including William Shatner and Lorne Greene, were killed off in the opening credits, while other visual gags, non sequiturs (unconnected and illogical statements used for comedic effect) and wordplay were used to supplement the frequently unusual action. The last shot was supposed to be a freeze frame but in reality only the actors held their positions while everything else around them (including escaping criminals) carried on as normal.

Despite being praised by the critics and earning two Emmy nominations, ABC axed the series after the fourth episode had aired. The reason given for the cancellation was that audiences had to concentrate too hard to appreciate all

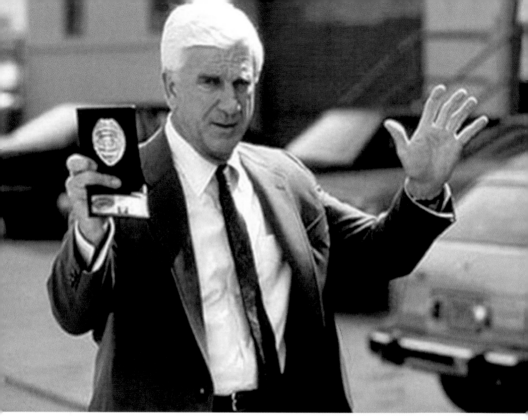

the audio and sight gags (many of which played out in the background), but this was seen as a cop out. The show was simply ahead of its time, which was highlighted by the success of the subsequent movies.

Nielsen reprised the role of Frank Drebin in *The Naked Gun*, although George Kennedy was cast as Hocken and OJ Simpson played Nordberg. Williams also returned as Ted Olson, while Priscilla Presley joined the cast as Frank's love interest, Jane Spencer. Between them, the three films grossed more than 200 million dollars.

The Professionals

The Professionals was a crime series from the pen of Brian Clemens, the creative force behind *The Avengers* and *The Persuaders*. It centred on the fictional CI5 (criminal intelligence) department of law enforcement, whose remit was to fight crime that was beyond the scope of everyday policing but which didn't involve the security services or the armed forces.

Gordon Jackson played the founder and head of the division, the no-nonsense George Cowley, while Martin Shaw and Lewis Collins played his two finest intelligence officers, Ray Doyle and William Bodie respectively. Cowley had a fine career as an officer in the British army before he joined the intelligence services. As head of CI5, he frequently came into conflict with Special Branch and MI5.

Ray Doyle was formerly a detective with the Derby police who then moved to East London. He's a diverse character who can handle himself in both armed and unarmed combat but who also immerses himself in art and music. He's bright and considerate but has a quick temper and often needs Bodie to come to his rescue.

Bodie left school at 14 and joined the merchant navy, although he ended up fighting as a mercenary in Africa. He then became a paratrooper who also served in the SAS before being recruited to CI5 by Cowley in the mid-1970s. Although equally competent with his fists, he was more relaxed and confident than his partner and preferred to use his wits to ease tension or to escape tricky situations.

The series relied on a healthy dose of action to supplement the dialogue, but some critics thought there was too much

violence and gun crime. Both Shaw and Collins did much of their own stunt work – particularly the driving and fight sequences, which drew further criticism for their comedic style. It also attracted attention for its political incorrectness, with frequent sexist, homophobic and racist language, although the dialogue was contemporary and wasn't initially viewed as disparaging to minority groups. Indeed the dialogue was only used when central to the plot, which was unlike the liberal use of controversial language in similar dramas like *The Sweeney*.

The series may have had its critics but it was a commercial success and ran for five series and 57 episodes between 1977 and 1983. Numerous cop shows copied the style and format throughout the 1980s, although attempts to revive three of the most popular characters on British television in the intervening years have all failed. The show remains popular in Germany and the Czech Republic, however, where it immediately achieved cult status.

Remington Steele

The idea for *Remington Steele* – a detective agency run by a woman – was first proposed by TV director Robert Butler in 1969. The premise was rejected because it was ahead of its time but, by the early 1980s, the success of several female-oriented sitcoms like the *Mary Tyler Moore Show* forced Grant Tinker at MTM to reconsider. Michael Gleason was drafted in to rework the premise but NBC still refused to take it on. Only when Tinker left for NBC was he in position to order a pilot.

Stephanie Zimbalist was cast as Laura Holt, a licensed private detective who can't get enough work because clients won't hire a female investigator. She gets round the problem by inventing a fictitious boss, Remington Steele (played by Pierce Brosnan). In the first episode, Brosnan's character, a former criminal whose real name is never divulged, assumes Steele's identity. Despite their public personas, Holt is the driving force at the agency and remains in charge.

Zimbalist initially rejected the role for fear of being tied to one show, and executives considered Brosnan an unwise choice as he was largely unknown in America, but both eventually grew into the roles and the series became extremely popular. Holt's performance in particular was praised for her strength, intelligence and independence. Despite rumours of off-screen discord, the chemistry between the pair allowed the writers to explore genres from romantic comedy to film noir to detective drama, and their relationship was to some extent aped by characters in later shows like *Moonlighting*.

The series was cancelled in 1985 despite having 28% of the audience share

REMINGTON STEELE and LAURA HOLT

REMINGTON STEELE

in its allocated time slot. NBC were forced to reverse their decision when ratings went even higher and fans protested the cancellation. This meant that Brosnan had to turn down the offer to play James Bond in *The Living Daylights*, although he took over from Timothy Dalton in time to play the part in *GoldenEye* (1995).

Remington Steele wound down with several TV movies in 1987. By then the series appeared to have run its course, although 94 episodes eventually aired.

The Saint

The Saint began life as a detective series that gradually morphed into a spy thriller in the James Bond mould. Novelist Leslie Charteris created the character of Simon Templar —his initials explain how the name of his alter ego was derived – in the 1920s. Roger Moore had always expressed a desire to play the part if the books were ever adapted for the screen, and he actually tried to acquire the rights himself. Before he became co-owner of the show with Robert Baker, he had been asked to try for the part.

The first few shows were based on Charteris's novels but original scripts had to be written as the series gained popularity. Although these took the Saint to more exotic locations, almost all of the filming took place at Elstree Studios in Hertfordshire. The show was one of the first to make the crossover from black and white to colour, with the first two production runs (71 episodes between 1962 and 1966) being shot in the former and the next two runs (47 episodes between 1967 and 1969) in colour. The first runs were so popular in the US that NBC gave it a primetime slot. It eventually aired in 60 countries and made ITV a profit of more than £350 million, making it one of the most successful shows of its kind.

The Saint introduced a number of props, such as the iconic white Volvo P1800, and also broke the 'fourth wall' in that Moore often addressed the audience directly. Cubby Broccoli and Harry Saltzman were so impressed with his performance that they repeatedly tried to lure him to the big screen to play James Bond, but Moore was tied to the series and felt that Connery was still the right

man for the job.

When Moore eventually took the role of 007 it seemed as if audiences had seen the last of the Saint, but Ian Ogilvy brought Simon Templar back to the small screen in 1978. The latest incarnation only lasted 24 episodes, however. In 1989 Simon Dutton starred in six feature-length stories, and Val Kilmer took on the role for a Hollywood version that bore little resemblance to the original character in 1997.

Silent Witness

Former detective Nigel McCrery created *Silent Witness*, a BBC crime series that follows a team of forensic pathologists, in 1996. He drew on inspiration from his own work on murder cases and based the original series on Professor Helen Witwell, one of his colleagues in the police force. Between 1996 and 2004, Amanda Burton played the lead character, Sam Ryan.

The first three series followed Ryan as she returned to Cambridge to pursue a teaching role while also working for the local police. The show has been criticised for its graphic and harrowing nature, and for taking liberties with forensic pathology, but audiences have remained loyal and it still attracts millions of viewers. It has also proved popular in the US and around the world, particularly in Scandinavia.

When Amanda Burton left at the end of the seventh series, Emilia Fox took over the lead female role as Doctor Nikki Alexander. Tom Ward played Doctor Harry Cunningham from series 6-15, while William Gaminara starred as Professor Leo Dalton until the character sacrificed himself to save his colleagues from a terrorist's bomb in the season finale to series 16. Fox now relies on David Caves, Liz Carr and Richard Lintern for support.

SOKO 5113

SOKO 5113 is one of the longest-running police procedural dramas. Originally conceived in 1976, first aired in 1978 and based in Munich, the German show broadcast its 500th episode at the end of its 38th season in 2013. The series is based on the memoirs of Kriminaldirektor (head of criminal investigations) Dieter Schenk who retired in 1975 and whose phone extension was 5113.

Schenk's police experience was so extensive that he wrote the screenplays for the series until 1986, after which he was retained by the production team as a consultant. His technique for bringing the stories (most of which involved organised crime) to life was to keep the characters and action as close to reality as possible. Cases were often left unsolved, for example, and there was great emphasis on factual forensic accuracy, the importance of teamwork, and detailed examination about how the characters interacted and how their private lives affected their careers.

Werner Kriendl was chosen to play Detective Inspector Karl Gottmann in the original series, and he remained in the role until his death in 1992. He was replaced at the head of the investigation team by Wilfried Klaus, who played Kriminalhauptkommissar Horst Schickl in 391 episodes between 1978 and 2009. When Schickl decided to change his identity and retire, Arthur Bauer (played by Gerd Silberbauer) took over as lead investigator, although he still answers to Detective Chief Commissioner Katharina Hahn and Chief Inspector Theo Renner.

Such has been the success of the series that it has spawned seven SOKO spinoffs and nine feature films. It remains one of the most popular German programs ever made.

Starsky & Hutch

Starsky & Hutch became one of the most popular cop shows of the 1970s. Created by William and Ryan Blinn, and starring David Soul as Ken 'Hutch' Hutchinson and Paul Michael Glaser as David Starsky, the series combined police procedural with buddy cop drama. It also broke the mould by giving major roles to African Americans (Antonio Fargas played Huggy Bear, a streetwise but ethically questionable informant, and Bernie Hamilton played the tough but fair captain of the fictional Bay City PD, Harold Dobey) at a time when on-screen stereotyping and off-screen discrimination were still prevalent in an American society divided by civil rights issues.

ABC commissioned the first series in 1975, but there was immediate criticism of the brotherly gestures of affection between Starsky and Hutch. While such camaraderie is considered normal today, in the mid-1970s it saw the pair labelled as 'primetime homos', so the back-slapping body language was toned down in later series. However, by then it was drawing criticism for the increasing level of violence. Glaser was so concerned that he threatened to leave the show unless more socially acceptable themes were explored in the plotlines. This didn't stop him continuing to voice his concern over the quality of the product, and he only agreed to stay on when granted more creative control over the scripts, guest spots as director and a pay rise from $5,000 to $35,000 per episode.

The enduring image from the series has nothing to do with its stars however. The red and white Ford Gran Torino became one of the most famous screen cars in history

after it debuted in the pilot. When producer Aaron Spelling first showed Glaser the car, the actor was distinctly underwhelmed, claiming it was big, ugly and childish, and that it would never be used by two undercover cops. David Soul was equally disparaging, saying it looked like a striped tomato. The nickname stuck and was eventually worked into the script whenever Hutch wanted to wind up his partner.

Despite its size and apparent power and speed, the Gran Torino was an unwieldy and lacklustre brute to drive. High performance engine notes were dubbed over the original rumbling, while modifications had to be made to the chassis and suspension to get the car to behave during the stunt sequences.

By 1979 Glaser had become so frustrated with the direction the show was taking that he walked at the end of its fourth season. Increasing production costs and declining ratings also contributed to the show's demise but it still ran to 93 episodes and spawned several similar buddy cop shows. Soul and Glaser had cameo parts in the hugely successful 2004 action comedy starring Ben Stiller as Starsky, Owen Wilson as Hutch and Snoop Dogg as Huggy Bear.

The Sweeney

The Sweeney was a British drama based on the Metropolitan Police's Flying Squad, the branch dealing with violent crime in the capital. It ran for four series and 53 episodes between 1975 and 1978 and starred John Thaw as DI Jack Regan and Dennis Waterman as DS George Carter.

The show initially aired as a pilot in 1974, although it only starred Thaw as Regan. Good ratings convinced ITV that Ian Kennedy Martin's premise had potential but he walked away from the project when producer Ted Childs insisted the show focus on outdoor action sequences rather than studio-based dialogue scenes.

The writers worked to a strict formula and ended up developing perhaps the first realistic urban crime drama shown on British television: the characters were fallible, usually brutal in their treatment of aggressive criminals and were occasionally happy to bend the law to secure an arrest. Regan in particular was a non-nonsense copper from Manchester who drank and smoked. He was happy to wade into trouble knowing that his fists would usually get him out of it, and he would often fabricate evidence, illegally enter property and use brute force to extract confessions. Despite this, he refused to break the law for personal gain and only cut corners in a professional capacity.

Carter was a former boxer whose training and discipline schooled him to avoid confrontation where possible, although he was handy with his fists when necessary. He's a football fan who's also a drinker and, after the death of his wife at the hands of a gang of diamond

smugglers, a serial womaniser.

The series proved so popular that guest stars like Joss Ackland, Lynda Bellingham, Brian Blessed, Simon Callow, Diana Dors, George Cole, John Hurt, Maureen Lipman, and Morecambe and Wise were all given roles. Two feature films were released between the third and fourth series, but the subsequent run suffered from personnel changes and weaker scripts so Thaw and Waterman decided to leave while it was still popular rather than risk it running out of ideas.

The Sweeney (which was actually rhyming slang – Sweeney Todd, Flying Squad) made a comeback in 2012 with a blockbuster movie starring Ray Winstone as Regan and Ben Drew as Carter.

Taggart

Taggart was a Scottish detective drama that was originally set in Glasgow at the fictional John Street Police Station, although some episodes were based in Edinburgh or the Highlands. It was created by Glenn Chandler, an award-winning playwright and novelist who devised a gritty and realistic urban police series that drew inspiration from actual events, people and locales.

Detective Chief Inspector Jim Taggart first appeared on screen in the BAFTA-winning pilot that was broadcast in 1983. Mark McManus's performance was praised as he brought a refreshing dynamism to a tough and cynical but sensitive role. His original partner, played by Neil Duncan, was Detective Sergeant Peter Livingstone, a graduate who had just joined the force. The interplay between the pair brought tension and drama to the roles as their relationship was often strained. When Duncan left the series in 1989, Taggart found himself with a female sidekick, Jackie Reid (played by Blythe Duff).

The series was at the peak of its popularity in 1994 when McManus died of pneumonia brought on by liver failure. He had suffered the loss of his second wife, his mother, brother and two sisters in the years before his death and had been drinking heavily. The character's funeral was aired in the final show of the 11th season. Michael Jardine (played by James MacPherson) then became the new DCI. Many thought the series wouldn't survive without its title character but the writers promoted DC Stuart Fraser (Colin McCredie), who then became the long-suffering partner, and ratings remained high.

Then, after 27 series and 109 episodes, the ITV network, which included Scottish Television, decided to pull the plug on one of the longest-running police dramas. The series had helped launch the careers of countless stars and was broadcast around the world, but, much to the disappointment of fans, it was deemed to have run its course and the final show aired in 2010.

T.J. Hooker

T.J. Hooker was an American police drama set in Los Angeles. It was created by Rick Husky whose credits also included *Walker, Texas Ranger*, a popular crime drama that starred Chuck Norris and ran for eight years and 203 episodes. *T.J. Hooker* was to have been a rehash of a former cop show but the pilot saw audiences warm to William Shatner's character, so the series was commissioned on the condition that it focused on Thomas Jefferson Hooker.

Hooker was formerly a beat cop so, when his partner was killed during a routine night patrol, Hooker resigned his position and returned to the role of uniformed policeman to rid the streets of crime. In the pilot, Hooker trained up a group of recruits, after which he was usually partnered with Vince Romano (played by Adrian Zmed). Hooker was forced to keep tabs on the brash youngster but the two eventually forged a good working relationship.

In the second series, the writers introduced the daughter of Station Captain Dennis Sheridan, Stacy, played by the darling of the mass media, Heather Locklear. The series quickly became one of the most watched on television and claimed a vast following, particularly amongst adolescent boys. Notable guest stars included Robert Davi, Jerry Lee Lewis, Sharon Stone and Tori Spelling.

The first four seasons were broadcast by ABC but, when they cancelled the show in 1985, it then switched to a later slot on CBS for a final series. Despite being popular around the world, CBS couldn't halt declining ratings and the show was axed after the 91st episode in 1986.

Van der Valk

Van der Valk was a British crime series set in Amsterdam. It centred on the characters and mood from Nicolas Freeling's novels, although none of his plots were actually used. Commissaris Simon 'Piet' van der Valk (played by Barry Foster) was a cynical but insightful detective whose cases usually involved the seedier side of the city. However unpleasant the crimes involving sex, drugs and murder were, the series was beautifully shot at the Thames Television studios in London and on location in the Netherlands. The detective was ably assisted by Inspecteur Johnny Kroon (Michael Latimer) and his superior, Hoofd-commissaris Samson (initially Nigel Stock and then Ronald Hines).

The first six episodes aired in 1972 and it showed enough promise to be recommissioned for a second series the following year. It returned in 1977 for a longer run. This was filmed more on location by Euston Films whose previous credits included *The Sweeney* and *Minder*. It therefore had a darker and more urban feel. The show then disappeared from screens until 1991, when four two-hour episodes were broadcast. It returned for a final season the following year.

The theme tune (*Eye Level*) proved immensely popular and the Simon Park Orchestra version reached the top of the UK singles chart in 1973. Matt Monro also took a vocal version into the charts later that year. In all, 32 episodes were filmed across the five series, although the show itself spanned 20 years.

Waking the Dead

Waking the Dead was a British crime drama focusing on the lives of a forensic unit investigating cold cases. Creator Barbara Machin drew a group of characters (police officers, psychologists and forensic investigators) and presented them with unsolved cases (usually murders).

Detective Superintendent Peter Boyd (Trevor Eve) led the team, and he was supported by psychological profiler Grace Foley (Sue Johnston), DI Spencer Jordan (Wilbert Johnson) as well as several additional characters. Boyd's motivation to tackle cold cases stemmed from the disappearance and murder of his son. Unable to come to terms with his grief, he was emotionally scarred and often beat suspects in fits of rage.

Jordan became Boyd's sidekick and the pair developed into the classic 'good cop-bad cop' partnership, with Jordan providing the softer touch in the interview room when Boyd was losing control. Foley's attention to detail, cool authority and vast experience provided the counterpoint to Boyd, although the pair enjoyed a close professional relationship. The writers incorporated domestic difficulties for all of the main cast to ensure the series remained credible and provided depth to their character.

After nine seasons and 92 episodes, Eve said that he wanted to move on. Rather than risk filming another series that might not be as well received, the BBC wisely wrapped it up while it was still popular and being broadcast around the world. The corporation then, unwisely as it turned out, filmed a spinoff focusing on the life and cases of forensic scientist Eve Lockhart (Tara Fitzgerald). *The Body Farm* was panned by critics and was shelved after a single series.

The Wire

The Wire was an American crime drama created by author and former police reporter David Simon (*Homicide: Life on the Street*). Set in Baltimore, each series centred on a different aspect of crime in the city, from the drug trade to government bureaucracy, from the education system to the media. It has been praised for its gritty urban realism and for its exploration of the fragility and interconnectedness of society.

It boasted a large cast of disparate characters but the emphasis was always on how they interacted. Simon was credited with refusing to allow big stars have key roles so that the stories and themes in the show wouldn't be overshadowed. He also insisted that the cast was largely African-American as that reflected the city's demographic. Lance Reddick was eventually chosen to play Cedric Daniels, while Michael Williams got the part of Omar Little. To give the show an authentic feel, many politicians, police officers and local personalities had small parts playing themselves despite not being trained performers.

Simon, who had a unique knowledge of the city having written for the *Baltimore Sun*, and co-writer Ed Burns (a veteran police officer with the Baltimore PD) drew on their experiences of life on the street to give the show a realism not found in mainstream dramas. As well as using contemporary language for both the law and criminals, some of the police were not driven to act for the greater good but because they believed they were better than the suspects, a situation which the writers maintain existed within the force.

Despite not winning many awards, the first season received positive reviews

from critics, and many neutrals compared it favourably with HBO's flagship drama, *The Sopranos*. The public didn't seem to get it, however, so viewing figures were relatively poor. This was blamed on the excessive use of street slang, the complexity of the storylines and a poor time slot in the schedule. Although broadcasters around the world also took it on, and Barack Obama named it his favourite show, *The Wire* was axed in 2008 after five seasons and 60 episodes.

Z-Cars

Z-*Cars* was a British police drama set in the fictional Newtown on Merseyside. Creators Troy Kennedy Martin (*The Italian Job*, *Kelly's Heroes*) and Allan Prior (*Softly, Softly*, *Blake's Seven*) chose the name not from the Ford Zephyr, which was the standard police patrol car, but from the fact that constabularies in Britain were each labelled with a letter and Z was then redundant.

They devised a series that focused on a different pair of officers each week. It was initially criticised by the police for the unsympathetic portrayal of officers but, with scripts that dealt with real issues, the public lapped it up. At a time when most police shows were based on the Met in London, the northern setting and regional flavour helped it stand apart.

The only character present during the entire run of 803 episodes between 1962 and 1978 was Bert Lynch (played by James Ellis), although several minor characters returned sporadically during the run of 12 series. Actors such as Brian Blessed, Leonard Rossiter, George Sewell, John Challis, Joss Ackland, John Thaw and Davy Jones of the Monkees also appeared.

When the original run ended in 1965, the characters of Inspector Barlow (Stratford Johns), Detective Sergeant Watt (Frank Windsor) and Sergeant Blackitt (Robert Keegan) were given their own drama series, *Softly, Softly*, which was based in the Bristol area. This BBC-produced, Ridley Scott-directed crime drama ran for 120 episodes between 1966 and 1969. The majority of the first two series of the spinoff were broadcast live (one of the last shows to do this), although by 1967 most episodes were

pre-recorded. When the BBC switched to colour transmissions in 1969, the series relocated to London and was rebranded *Softly, Softly: Taskforce*. It ran for another seven years and 149 episodes.

The BBC's preference for live filming and erasing tapes afterwards means that only around 320 episodes of *Z-Cars* remain in their archives. It is still considered a seminal series in that it was frequently imitated but never bettered. Even the theme music charted in the UK and it has since been adopted by Everton, Tranmere and Watford football clubs.

Cop Shows Quiz: Questions

1. Who was the original host of America's Most Wanted?

2. On whose novels was A Touch of Frost based?

3. Where was Bergerac set?

4. Who played Burnside in The Bill?

5. Which member of the Reagan family was killed by corrupt police in Blue Bloods?

6. Where in Australia was Blue Heelers based?

7. Who played Dr Temperance Brennan in Bones?

8. How many Emmy Awards did Cagney & Lacey win?

9. Which ITV police drama preceded C.A.T.S. Eyes?

10. Which member of Charlie's Angels married Lee Majors?

11. Whose novels inspired the television adaptation of Charlie Chan?

12. Who played Francis 'Ponch' Poncherello in CHiPs?

13. For which city's police department did homicide detective Lilly Rush work in the show Cold Case?

14. Which two major stars turned down the role of Columbo?

15. Who created Cracker?

16. How many viewers watched The Big Game episode of American drama Criminal Minds?

17. What does CSI stand for?

18. Who played Detective Inspector Peter Pascoe in Dalziel & Pascoe?

19. Where did James Dempsey come from in Dempsey and Makepeace?

20. How many episodes were there of Dixon of Dock Green?

21. Which American network initially broadcast Dragnet?

22. For which two films did Due South creator Paul Haggis win Academy Awards?

23. What was the name of the police officer charged with involuntary manslaughter during the filming of The First 48?

24. Who played Detective Chief Superintendent Christopher Foyle in Foyle's War?

25. Who played the one-armed man in the 1993 film adaptation of The Fugitive?

26. Who write the theme tune to Hawaii Five-0?

27. In which fictional Yorkshire town was Heartbeat set?

28. How many Emmy nominations did Hill Street Blues earn?

29. Who wrote the Inspector Gently stories that inspired the TV series?

30. Which car did Inspector Morse drive?

31. Who played both Ironside and Perry Mason?

32. In which fictional town was Juliet Bravo set?

33. Who did George Savalas play in Kojak?

34. Who created Law & Order?

35. What was the name of the beachfront estate in Magnum P.I.?

36. What colour was the Ferrari Testarossa in the original TV series of Miami Vice?

37. Neil Dudgeon played John Barnaby in Midsomer Murders, but in which Renée Zellweger film did he have a bit part as a taxi driver?

38. What is the movie-industry term for when the actors address the audience or the crew play bit parts to supplement the action, such as in the hit comedy-drama Moonlighting?

39. What does MCRT stand for in the hit American show NCIS?

40. How many years did NYPD Blue run for?

41. In which Hollywood blockbuster did David Suchet play the villainous Nagi Hassan?

42. Why was Police Camera Action! taken off air for three years?

43. The team behind the spoof Police Squad! wrote and directed which film starring Val Kilmer as pop star Nick Rivers?

44. When Pierce Brosnan was refused permission to leave Remington Steele to play James Bond, who did Cubby Broccoli choose instead?

45. Which car did Ian Ogilvy drive in Return of The Saint?

46. Who wrote the theme tune to Silent Witness?

47. Where is SOKO 5113 based?

48. Who played the villain in the 2004 Hollywood version of Starsky & Hutch?

49. Dennis Waterman played ex-boxer George Carter in The Sweeney, but he had a similar role as which character in Minder?

50. T.J. Hooker's Heather Locklear has been married to which two rock stars?

Cop Shows Quiz: Answers

1. John Walsh

2. R.D. Wingfield

3. Jersey

4. Christopher Ellison

5. Joseph / Joe

6. Mount Thomas, Victoria

7. Emily Deschanel

8. 14

9. The Gentle Touch

10. Farrah Fawcett

11. Earl Derr Biggers

12. Erik Estrada

13. Philadelphia

14. Lee Cobb and Bing Crosby

15. Jimmy McGovern

16. 26 million

17. Crime Scene Investigation

18. Colin Buchanan

19. New York

20. 432

21. NBC

22. Million Dollar Baby and Crash

23. Joseph Weekley

24. Michael Kitchen

25. Andreas Katsulas

26. Morton Stevens

27. Ashfordly

28. 98

29. Alan Hunter

30. 1960 Mark 2 Jaguar

31. Raymond Burr

32. Hartley

33. Sergeant Heathcliff 'Fatso' Stavros

34. Dick Wolf

35. Robin's Nest

36. White

37. Bridget Jones: The Edge of Reason

38. Breaking the fourth wall

39. Major Case Response Team

40. 12 (1993-2005)

41. Executive Decision

42. Presenter Alastair Stewart had been convicted of drink-driving

TAGGART

**The pictures in this book were provided
courtesy of the following:**

WIKICOMMONS
commons.wikimedia.org

Design & Artwork by Scott Giarnese

Published by Demand Media Limited

Publishers: Jason Fenwick & Jules Gammond

Written by Liam McCann